GW01325868

Original title:
Winter's Reflection

Author: Kätriin Kaldaru
ISBN HARDBACK: 978-9916-79-726-6
ISBN PAPERBACK: 978-9916-79-727-3
ISBN EBOOK: 978-9916-79-728-0

A Whisper from the Other Side of Winter

Soft winds carry tales untold,
As shadows fade in twilight's hold.
The world is hushed, wrapped in white,
A promise stirs within the night.

Each flake a dream, a fleeting sigh,
Beneath the sky where whispers lie.
Hope flickers on the edge of dawn,
With warmth returning, winter's gone.

The Crystalline Heart of Solitude

Amidst the stillness, silence speaks,
In frosted breath where longing peaks.
The heart, encased in icy sheen,
Yearns for a touch, a sight unseen.

Stars blink like secrets in the dark,
A solitary ember's spark.
In the depths, a flame can grow,
Though crystal walls may steal the glow.

Frigid Hearts and Warmth of Memory

In corners cold where echoes stay,
Frozen whispers drift away.
Yet in the heart, the embers gleam,
Through frigid nights, a vibrant dream.

Faces of old, like shadows dance,
Memory's warmth, a fleeting chance.
Though time may chill with bitter breath,
Love's flame survives, defying death.

Ghostly Forms in a Lantern Glow

Beneath the glow of lanterns' light,
Wraiths of the past emerge from night.
They flicker soft, like candle's flame,
In whispers shared, they call my name.

Their laughter lingers on the breeze,
A haunting dance among the trees.
In shadows deep, they weave their tale,
Of lost embraces, love's sweet veil.

Serenity Wrapped in Midnight's Chill

The stars quilt the night so bright,
Whispers of dreams take gentle flight.
Moonlight dances on silver streams,
Wrapped in the hush of midnight dreams.

Cool breezes sigh through ancient trees,
Rustling leaves sing soft melodies.
A tranquil heart in nature's fold,
Finds peace in stories yet untold.

Darkness cradles the world in grace,
Each shadow holds a sacred space.
In stillness, life's wonders reveal,
The calmness that the night can seal.

Time slows down beneath the skies,
Whispers of hope in starlit sighs.
Serenity cloaked in midnight's chill,
Invites the soul to be still.

Beneath this shroud of velvet night,
The heart beats softly, pure delight.
Wrapped in serenity's warm embrace,
We find our refuge, our sacred place.

Through the Crystal Veil of Night

Beyond the horizon, the stars align,
A vision unfolds, so rare, divine.
Through the crystal veil, shadows play,
Guiding lost souls along their way.

The moon, a lantern, casts its gaze,
Illuminating the twilight haze.
In quiet corners, secrets dwell,
Stories linger, waiting to tell.

Stillness wraps the earth in peace,
As time and troubles gently cease.
Echoes of laughter drift afar,
In the embrace of the evening star.

From twilight's edge to dawn's first light,
Hope ignites within the night.
Through the crystal veil, dreams take wing,
A symphony of life, we sing.

The night is alive with vibrant hues,
A canvas painted in deep blues.
Through the crystal veil, life feels bright,
In the calm embrace of endless night.

The Quiet Beneath the Snow

Whispers float on frosty air,
Blankets soft, a world laid bare.
Footprints pause, the silence sings,
Nature's hush, the peace it brings.

Frosted dreams in twilight glow,
Stillness wrapped in purest snow.
Time stands still in winter's grip,
As softly, snowflakes gently slip.

Bare Trees and Bone-Cold Breezes

Branches stretch with aching grace,
Against the wind, they find their place.
Cold breath whispers through the night,
Lonely silhouettes in fading light.

Leaves once danced, now memories stay,
Echoes of warmth, now far away.
Frozen trunks, a forest bare,
Haunted by forgotten care.

Shards of Crystal Memories

Twinkling lights like stars in time,
Fractured moments, held in rhyme.
Each fragment tells a tale once shared,
Fragments of love, preserved and spared.

Frozen laughter, joy displayed,
Glittering dreams that never fade.
In the depths of winter's chill,
Hearts remember, and always will.

Shadows Cast by Glacial Glow

In twilight's hush, shadows creep,
Glacial gleam where secrets sleep.
Cold reflections on the ground,
In their depths, lost tales are found.

Flickering lights from distant shores,
Whispered tales of ancient wars.
Echoes soft, the night unfolds,
Mysteries in the moonlight told.

Memories Wrapped in a White Veil

Soft whispers float in the air,
Frozen echoes of days gone by.
Each flake a story, tender and rare,
Brought forth beneath the pale sky.

Gentle shadows dance on the ground,
In the hush of twilight's embrace.
With each breath, love's warmth is found,
As snowflakes fall with delicate grace.

Wrapped in silence, time stands still,
Moments cherished, yet bittersweet.
In the chill, memories fulfill,
Each winter's tale, a soft heartbeat.

Frosted dreams in a soft white shroud,
Yearning whispers call from the past.
In nature's beauty, we stand proud,
Making memories meant to last.

In the glow of the fading light,
Hope sparkles like snow on a tree.
Wrapped in this silence, pure and bright,
Our hearts unite in harmony.

Hushed Tides of a Frosty Dusk

The river's breath is cold as night,
Embracing shadows, calm and deep.
Stars awaken, twinkling light,
As nature rests in silent sleep.

Frosty fingers touch the shore,
A blanket whispers of the past.
Echoes linger, forevermore,
Hushed tides sing a song so vast.

Moonbeams shimmer on icy waves,
Reflecting secrets lost in time.
In the stillness, the heart braves,
Waves of nostalgia, sweet and prime.

Branches bow with a tender sigh,
Crystals gleaming in twilight's glow.
The chilly air, a soft goodbye,
Nature's canvas wrapped in snow.

As dusk fades into soft twilight,
Dreams float softly on winter's breath.
In this frosty, gentle night,
Life embraces both life and death.

Veils of Ice and Forgotten Tales

Frozen whispers drape the trees,
Veils of ice glimmering bright.
Each branch captures the winter's breeze,
Storing secrets in the night.

Stories linger within the frost,
Unfolding slowly, one by one.
The beauty stirs, though time is lost,
With each dawn, new dreams begun.

Curled beneath a soft white sheet,
Olden tales of love and strife.
Nature's quiet, rhythmic beat,
Reflects the dance of fleeting life.

Silhouettes against twilight's glow,
Whispering echoes ride the chill.
Veils of ice, the stories flow,
Remembered in the heart's own thrill.

As day breaks soft and light returns,
Frosted patterns will softly fade.
Yet in our hearts, the longing burns,
For every tale that winter made.

Crystal Ornaments on Nature's Canvas

Nature drapes a sparkling veil,
Crystal ornaments lace the trees.
Each branch a story, soft and frail,
Dancing gently in the breeze.

Sunlight kisses every flake,
A mosaic crafted with care.
In this winter wonder, we wake,
Magic lingers in the air.

Frozen patterns, intricate, bold,
Each moment captured, crystal clear.
Nature's artistry unfolds,
A masterpiece for all to hear.

Silent whispers in the snow,
Stories woven in each crest.
Threads of wonder start to glow,
In this canvas, we find rest.

At the close of day, they gleam,
A spectacle of winter's grace.
In our hearts, we hold the dream,
Of nature's beauty, pure embrace.

The Solstice's Encased Glow

The night sky dances bright,
Stars twinkle, a soft sight.
Whispers of warmth arise,
In winter's calm, surprise.

Frost blankets every tree,
Nature's art, wild and free.
In the stillness, we find,
Magic woven, entwined.

Candles flicker in the dark,
Filling hearts with hope's spark.
The world slows down to dream,
In this moment, we beam.

Beneath the moon's soft glare,
We feel the cosmic air.
Time slips through our embrace,
In winter's warm, safe space.

Poised Beneath an Icy Canopy

Trees stand tall, cloaked in white,
Boughs heavy, a stunning sight.
Snowflakes glimmer, softly fall,
Nature's blanket covers all.

Silence wraps the world around,
In this hush, peace can be found.
Breath turns into crystal mist,
As we pause, we can't resist.

Ice forms art on window panes,
Capturing winter's soft refrains.
A symphony of chilly air,
Reminds us life is always there.

The earth sleeps, a tranquil scene,
Beneath the icy, frosted sheen.
Yet within this still domain,
Life awaits, a vibrant vein.

A Palette of Frozen Echoes

Colors fade to shades of white,
Nature's canvas, pure delight.
Brush of frost paints every place,
A tranquil, breathtaking space.

Echoes of laughter and cheer,
Resound in the chilly air near.
Children dance, their breath like steam,
Chasing shadows in a dream.

Berries pop with colors bright,
Amidst the snowy, gentle night.
Textures blend, a feast for eyes,
In this world, where magic lies.

Footprints left upon the ground,
Mark the joy that we have found.
Each step tells a story true,
In frozen hues, we break through.

Dreams Nested in Crystal Whispers

Whispers float on winter's breeze,
Lulled by the rustling trees.
Dreams take form in gentle sighs,
In the chill, imagination flies.

Moonlight bathes the world in glow,
Casting dreams on falling snow.
Each flake carries a soft tale,
Of hopes and wishes, sweet and frail.

In this tranquil, quiet night,
Hearts lift in the pale starlight.
Crystals dance in shadows deep,
Promising secrets they will keep.

Nestled close, we find our peace,
As frosty breaths begin to cease.
Held in dreams, both vast and wide,
In winter's magic, we abide.

Nightfall's Cold Caress

The sun dips low, the shadows creep,
In twilight's arms, the world will sleep.
Stars emerge, a sparkling trace,
Nightfall wraps in cold caress.

Whispers linger in the air,
Ghostly shapes beyond compare.
Moonlight dances, soft and bright,
Guiding dreams through endless night.

The chill of night, a fleeting kiss,
In silver glow, find fleeting bliss.
Crickets sing their evening song,
As time drifts by, both slow and long.

A gentle breeze stirs leaves to sway,
Carrying scents of end of day.
Stars align in silent cheer,
Nightfall's beauty, ever near.

Embrace the dark, let worries fade,
In night's embrace, find solace made.
For in this still, enchanted space,
Hearts entwine in nightfall's grace.

The Fire that Warms the Frozen Heart

Amidst the chill, a spark ignites,
Turning winter's grasp to bright delights.
A flicker burns within the soul,
Healing wounds, making us whole.

The embers glow, a tender hue,
Where once was cold, now warmth breaks through.
With every flame, old pains depart,
As fire whispers to the heart.

In every crackle, hope takes flight,
Chasing shadows from the night.
The heart, once frozen, now will dance,
In rhythm with this warm expanse.

Gather 'round and share this light,
Together we can face the night.
For in our unity, we find,
A fire that warms both heart and mind.

Though winter's chill may still persist,
This fire kindles love's sweet tryst.
A beacon bright, we'll stand our part,
Wrapped in warmth, a thawed-out heart.

Breaths of Red Embers and Frost

In twilight's breath, the embers glimmer,
While frost wraps trees, a crystal shimmer.
Fire and ice, a dance profound,
Nature's beauty all around.

The warmth of coals, a soft embrace,
Meets winter's chill in a tender race.
Each spark that flies, a story spun,
Of battles fought, and victories won.

Breathe in the contrast, so divine,
Where warmth and cool together intertwine.
Embers flicker, casting light,
Amongst the frost, a dazzling sight.

The night air whispers in crisp delight,
Breath of frost and embers bright.
In this moment, life unfolds,
A tapestry of warmth and cold.

So let us cherish every breath,
In hues of red and icy depth.
For life's a fire, both fierce and lost,
In breaths of red embers and frost.

Glistening Branches Beneath a Silver Moon

Glistening branches reach for the sky,
Cloaked in frost as night slips by.
A silver moon, its light bestowed,
Whispers secrets to the road.

Each leaf adorned with icy lace,
Reflecting dreams in a tranquil space.
The world, aglow in soft perfume,
Held within the moonlit room.

Beneath the stars, a blanket wide,
Nature hums and softly sighs.
Branches sway in gentle tune,
A lullaby beneath the moon.

In this quiet, magic brews,
With echoes of the heart's true hues.
We find our peace in nature's grip,
As the night takes a soothing trip.

So linger here, let moments flow,
Let all your worries cease to grow.
For beneath the silvering beam,
Life unfolds like a whispered dream.

Ghosts of Glimmers Past

In the shadows, whispers sigh,
Echoes of laughter drift on by.
Faded memories, soft and light,
Ghosts of glimmers, lost from sight.

Through the halls where shadows creep,
Worn-down secrets, buried deep.
Vows made under a silver moon,
Now just a haunting, old-time tune.

Pictures fade on yellowed walls,
Time unlocks and softly calls.
A dance of memories intertwined,
The ghosts of glimmers, undefined.

Yet still they linger, sweet and rare,
Fragments of joy float in the air.
Chasing light where hope was cast,
In the echoes, moments last.

In quiet corners, lost loves dwell,
In every heart, a hidden swell.
With each glance towards the past,
Ghosts of glimmers hold us fast.

The Quiet After the Storm

Silence drapes the battered ground,
In stillness now, no cries resound.
Trees stand tall, brushed by the sun,
The quiet after all is done.

Raindrops linger on leaves so green,
A glistening world, calm and serene.
The air is fresh, a sweet relief,
Wounds of nature find their brief.

Birds return with cheerful song,
Notes a promise we belong.
Bright blooms rise where shadows lay,
In the quiet, we find our way.

Footsteps soft on muddy trails,
Every heartbeat, nature hails.
In this moment, peace restored,
After the storm, love is poured.

Hope shines bright with colors bold,
In warm embrace, stories told.
From chaos comes a brand new start,
The quiet after heals the heart.

Frost-Covered Dreams Unfurled

A blanket white on fields so vast,
Whispers of winter, shadows cast.
Frosted dreams, like crystal lace,
In morning light, a tender grace.

Each breath a cloud, each step a thrill,
Nature pauses, time stands still.
A world transformed in icy sheen,
Frost-covered dreams, pure and serene.

Underneath, the earth sleeps deep,
With silent promise, secrets keep.
Yet through the chill, life gently stirs,
In quiet corners, warmth concurs.

Branches sparkle, a jeweled crown,
In the stillness, shadows drown.
Each glimmer holds a whispered name,
Frost-covered dreams, forever flame.

With every dawn, hope breaks anew,
In winter's grasp, the world feels true.
A tapestry of beauty swirled,
In frost-covered dreams unfurled.

In the Tender Grasp of Cold

Beneath the sky, a chill embraces,
Nature pauses, time retraces.
In the tender grasp of cold,
Silent tales of winter told.

Blankets thick on fields of white,
Stars above, a shimmering sight.
Winds that whisper secrets low,
In the tender grasp, joy will grow.

Footprints marked in snowy trails,
Each one tells of love that pales.
Yet in the cold, warmth we find,
Hearts entwined, forever kind.

Underneath a blanket dark,
Fires flicker, igniting spark.
Together, facing frosts and fears,
In the tender grasp, shed the tears.

So let the winter come and play,
In its embrace, we'll find our way.
Hand in hand, we brave the fold,
In the tender grasp of cold.

Stars Drifting in a Silver Sea

In the quiet night sky, they gleam,
Whispers of dreams in a silver beam.
Softly they dance on the ocean's crest,
Guiding lost souls to peaceful rest.

Ripples of light, a calm embrace,
Each star a story, a timeless grace.
Waves shimmer gently under their glow,
Secrets of the universe flow.

They twinkle and fade like a whispered sigh,
A canvas of wonder stretching high.
In the depths of night, their beauty shines,
A boundless world where hope entwines.

Stars drift softly, the sea will call,
In their silent dance, we feel so small.
Yet within their light, we find our place,
In the vastness of time, a warm embrace.

The Veil of Stillness

Beneath the hush of twilight's kiss,
A gentle calm, a tranquil bliss.
The world lies wrapped in a tender sigh,
As shadows stretch and soft winds fly.

Time stands still, a breath held tight,
In the moon's embrace, everything feels right.
Branches sway like silent prayers,
Whispers of peace hang in the airs.

The stars peep through the veil of night,
Illuminating dreams with silver light.
Each moment lingers, a fleeting pause,
In stillness, we find the heart's true cause.

Wrapped in silence, we drift along,
Carried by echoes of a soothing song.
In the depths of stillness, we find our way,
A soft reminder of love's sweet sway.

Frost-Kissed Wishes on the Breeze

In winter's breath, the world is gleamed,
Frosted whispers dance where sunlight streamed.
Each flake a wish, a gentle plea,
Carried on winds, wild and free.

Softly they twirl in the crisp, cool air,
Painting the earth with beauty rare.
Glistening dreams on branches sway,
Nature's canvas in frosty array.

In the hush of dawn, a sparkle bright,
Frost-kissed wishes in morning light.
Each breath we take, a pearl of ice,
A moment precious, a fleeting slice.

With every whisper, the heart takes flight,
Seeking the warmth, turning cold to light.
In this wintry spell, we find our ease,
Wrapped in the magic of frost-kissed breeze.

Ghosts of the Frigid Moonlight

In the pale glow of a midnight hue,
Ghostly whispers drift, ever anew.
Shadows flicker, they weave and glide,
Through the still night where secrets bide.

They whisper tales of forgotten dreams,
Echoes of love in silvery beams.
In the chill of night, their stories unfold,
Of heartbeats lost and yet retold.

Beneath the moon, they swirl and sway,
In the silence, they softly play.
Phantom moments in the air,
Lingering softly, a ghostly flare.

In the darkened sky, their dance takes form,
Guided by the light, they quietly swarm.
In this frigid world, they find their grace,
Ghosts of the night in a tender embrace.

Whispers of a Snowy Reverie

The snowflakes dance and swirl,
Silent whispers in the air,
Each one a fleeting pearl,
Winter's breath, cold and rare.

Beneath the trees they settle,
Soft coats of glistening white,
Nature's frozen mettle,
In the stillness of the night.

Footsteps crunch with gentle sound,
Voices low, a distant call,
In this world, we're tightly bound,
As winter wraps us, one and all.

Dreams unfold like paper kites,
Tethered to the chilling breeze,
Carried forth in chilly flights,
Silent tales among the trees.

The moonlight bathes the scene bright,
Casting shadows, crisp and clear,
In these whispers, pure delight,
Snowy reveries draw near.

Illuminated by the January Sun

A golden touch on icy ground,
January's warmth breaks through,
Each ray a promise, brightly found,
Nature painted in vibrant hue.

The world awakens from its slumber,
With sparkles dancing in the dew,
Hope ignites, a radiant number,
As the skies reveal their blue.

Trees stand tall, their branches bare,
Beneath the sun's embracing glow,
Winter fades in warmth's sweet care,
In every heart, the fire flows.

Birds begin their joyful song,
Celebrating life anew,
Echoes of a world so strong,
Illuminated, we pursue.

In this gentle, warming grace,
We find the strength to carry on,
With January's soft embrace,
We welcome spring with rising dawn.

Frosted Panes and Warmth Within

Frosted panes, a silvery lace,
Whispering tales of winter's chill,
Inside, a cozy, warm embrace,
The hearth aglow, the world stands still.

With every breath, the vapor glows,
A misty sign of warmth inside,
As outside, flurries gently pose,
Creating art where dreams abide.

Candles flicker, shadows dance,
In the corners where spirits play,
Each flick of light, a fleeting glance,
At moments lost, yet here to stay.

Sipping cocoa, laughter shared,
Wrapped in blankets, hearts alight,
In simple joys, we are prepared,
To face the cold, to chase the night.

Frosted panes, a world so vast,
Yet here within, we are complete,
Together, we can hold the fast,
In warmth and love, we find our seat.

Beneath the Blanket of the Night

Beneath the blanket of the night,
Stars like diamonds, twinkling bright,
The moon weaves tales of cool delight,
In shadows soft, the world feels right.

Whispers of the gentle breeze,
Carrying secrets from afar,
Rustling leaves with quiet ease,
In the dark, we find our star.

A distant owl calls out her song,
Echoing through the tranquil wood,
In this moment, we belong,
Where silence reigns and dreams feel good.

The night wraps all in velvet peace,
As time stands still, the heart takes flight,
In this embrace, our worries cease,
Beneath the blanket of the night.

Close your eyes, let visions roam,
In slumber's depth, we lose our way,
But under stars, we find our home,
In whispers soft, we drift away.

Frost-Kissed Traces of the Past

Whispers of winter brush the ground,
Ruins of memories softly found.
Footprints leading where shadows play,
In silence, the old tales sway.

Crystals sparkle in muted light,
Ghosts of laughter take to flight.
Beneath the frost, secrets hide,
In the chill, old hopes abide.

Echoes dance in the frosty air,
Promises made, now laid bare.
As the moon casts its gentle gaze,
We remember those fleeting days.

Time is frozen, yet still flows,
In the quiet, nostalgia grows.
Every flake a story told,
In icy silence, the past unfolds.

Chants of the Icebound Winds

Hollow howls in the frosty night,
Winds that carry the moon's pale light.
Songs of winter echo through trees,
Borne on currents, dancing with ease.

Voices whisper of tales long gone,
Through the branches, they travel on.
Chill caresses the breath of time,
In the stillness, a haunting rhyme.

Lament of nature, strong and free,
Notes of sorrow, wild and spree.
A symphony of ice and snow,
In harmony, the feelings flow.

Under the veil of a silver sky,
Resonant dreams, they soar and fly.
With every gust, the heart takes wing,
Chants of the icebound winter sing.

The Stillness That Covers All

In the silence, the world holds its breath,
A blanket of white is spun from death.
Stillness drapes over each familiar street,
Every echo's a memory, bittersweet.

Softly it falls, this winter's shroud,
Muffling voices, quieting the crowd.
Time slows down in this hushed embrace,
Nature's canvas, a glacial space.

Branches heavy with crystalline dreams,
Under the weight, the landscape gleams.
Lost in the moment, we find our peace,
The clamor fades, our worries cease.

Snowflakes flutter like whispered charms,
In their descent, they mean no harm.
As twilight blankets the frozen ground,
In the stillness, a joy profound.

Heartbeats Underneath a Shroud of Snow

Beneath the surface, life pulsates slow,
Hidden warmth where the chill winds blow.
Layers thick veil the dreams we weave,
In quiet moments, we learn to believe.

Frosty breath mingles with the dark,
Each heartbeat ignites a hidden spark.
In the blanket, hope continues to thrive,
In soft rhythms, the spirit's alive.

Snow patters down with a gentle sigh,
Covering whispers, the world slips by.
Yet underneath, a fire remains,
A pulse, a dance in winter's chains.

Awake in dreams where shadows blend,
A journey of heartbeats that never end.
Through the cold, our truths emerge,
Under the snow, we quietly surge.

The Heart's Wake in Frigid Air

In the stillness, whispers play,
Where the winter's breath holds sway.
A pulse beneath the frozen lake,
Awakens dreams that silence break.

Frosty tendrils gently creep,
Over surfaces where secrets sleep.
The heart beats strong, yet soft and slow,
In the chime of winter's soft, white glow.

Beneath the ice, a fire lies,
In hidden depths, it softly sighs.
Crystals form a tapestry,
Frigid beauty sets the spirit free.

Like whispers wrapped in satin cold,
The heart's warm stories finally told.
While breath hangs thick in icy air,
A dance of warmth, beyond despair.

In every flake, a tale unfolds,
Of love enduring, fierce and bold.
The heart's wake spreads, so bittersweet,
In frigid silence, where lovers meet.

Glacial Dreams and Quiet Starbursts

In dreams spun from ice and cold,
Glacial whispers, stories unfold.
Quiet starbursts in the night,
Each one holding a wish in flight.

Underneath a blanket white,
Awake the dreams, take to the light.
Frosted stars, they flicker and gleam,
Guiding paths through frozen streams.

A tapestry of icy lace,
In every corner, beauty's grace.
They glimmer soft, with tales untold,
In the heart of winter, brave and bold.

With every breath, the world holds still,
As joy and wonder slowly fill.
Frozen realms invite the brave,
To seek the warmth that dreams can save.

Together we cherish the silent glow,
In glacial dreams where the heart can flow.
Quiet starbursts light our way,
In the dance of night, where hopes sway.

Shadows Danced on Icy Lake

Underneath the silver moon,
Shadows glide, a whispered tune.
Dancing lightly, spirits play,
On the icy lake, where dreams lay.

Figures twist in frosty air,
An ethereal waltz, so rare.
Whispers mingle, soft and low,
In every shadow, love can grow.

Ripples form with every sway,
Casting dreams that drift away.
Echoes of a deeper night,
In twilight's kiss, they take their flight.

A canvas spread in hues so bright,
Shadows weave through the silent night.
With icy breath, the world feels near,
In this dance, we share no fear.

The icy lake, a timeless place,
Where shadows find their warm embrace.
Beneath the stars, our spirits break,
To dance on dreams and solitude's wake.

Breath of Frost, Embrace of Cold

Whispers of frost in twilight's haze,
Surround the heart with icy ways.
Each breath hangs heavy, crystal clear,
Embrace of cold, drawing near.

Morning breaks with silver rays,
Light dapples on the frozen lays.
A soft embrace that wraps the soul,
In winter's arms, we become whole.

Echoes of laughter on frosted ground,
In every moment, joy is found.
The breath of frost, a sacred bond,
With nature's touch, we feel so fond.

In every flake, a memory spun,
Of moments cherished, laughter won.
The heart beats loud, through cold we roam,
In winter's grip, we find our home.

Together we dance, hand in hand,
Two spirits warmed on this frozen land.
Every breath, a promise made,
In frost and cold, love won't fade.

Echoes of Warmth Amidst Prairies of Ice

In the hush of winter's breath,
Whispers dance through frozen grass.
Warmth flickers in the heart,
Amidst the snow's soft embrace.

Sunlight paints the icy seas,
Reflecting dreams that gently sway.
Echoes of laughter fill the breeze,
Melodies that will not fade.

Footsteps trace a path so bright,
As shadows weave through silver night.
Each step sends a spark of light,
Awakening the winter's might.

Branches bend with crystal weight,
Holding secrets that they keep.
Time stands still, no need to wait,
In this frozen world, we leap.

Beneath the stars, a warm glow gleams,
With echoes of our frozen dreams.
Together here, let souls unite,
In prairies vast, our hearts ignite.

The Blanket of Serene Silence

A blanket stitched from quiet grace,
Covers the earth in softest lace.
Snowflakes fall in gentle trails,
Silence sings as winds exhale.

Each flake tells a story bright,
Of winter's calm and starry night.
In hushed whispers, dreams take flight,
Wrapped in peace, the world feels right.

Beneath this coat of winter's peace,
All bustle fades, and worries cease.
With every breath, a soft release,
In this stillness, spirits feast.

The moonlight glimmers, cool and clear,
In this silence, we draw near.
Holding moments close and dear,
As hearts align, the world will cheer.

With every heartbeat, hope awakes,
In winter's hush, our warmth remakes.
In the silence, love will blaze,
A blanket woven from our gaze.

Luminous Crystals of a Wintry Tale

Crystals gleam like stars at dawn,
Whispers of magic softly drawn.
Each flake, a story yet untold,
In winter's heart, they brightly hold.

Frosted windows frame the scene,
Where dreams are woven, pure and keen.
Light dances on the snowy ground,
In this realm, pure beauty's found.

A tapestry of white and blue,
Painted skies, a wondrous view.
Each breath of air, a frosty kiss,
In the chill, we find our bliss.

Footprints mark the path we take,
Through sparkling fields and icy lake.
With every step, a tale unfolds,
In luminous crystals, secrets told.

And as the night begins to rise,
The moon, a pearl in velvet skies.
Wintry tales we softly share,
In frozen beauty, love is rare.

Shadows Lengthen in the Frosty Air

As daylight wanes, the shadows creep,
In frosty air, the silence deep.
Whispers of night begin to play,
In twilight's grasp, we softly sway.

The trees stand tall, their branches bare,
Holding secrets in cold air.
Every flicker of a dying light,
Promises warmth in winter's night.

A world draped in a silver hue,
Where dreams whisper, soft and true.
The chill bites gently at our cheeks,
In this quiet, comfort seeks.

Stars awaken, twinkling bright,
In the embrace of a velvet night.
Each one a wish upon the chill,
Through frosty air, our hearts stand still.

Together we find warmth in sight,
Shadows lengthen, hold us tight.
In frosty air, we're never alone,
In the embrace of winter's tone.

The Song of Bare Branches

In winter's grip, they stand so tall,
With silent whispers, they call.
Their limbs reach out, like hands in prayer,
A melody carried on frosty air.

The winds weave notes through every limb,
A haunting song, both soft and grim.
They sway and dance to nature's tune,
Beneath the watchful, pale-faced moon.

Each crack and creak tells tales of yore,
Of storms that raged and skies that tore.
Yet still they sing, in stark delight,
A testament to endurance's fight.

In time's embrace, they shed their fears,
And cradle dreams through silent years.
A symphony of strength and grace,
In the winter's calm, they find their place.

A Palette of Crystal Blue and White

In morning light, the world awakes,
With shades of blue and ice-like flakes.
A canvas bright, so pure and clear,
Where dreams of winter reappear.

The sky adorned in gentle hues,
While snowflakes waltz, the earth they choose.
Each breath of air, a whispered song,
Inviting hearts to come along.

The frozen lake, a mirror wide,
Reflecting all the skies abide.
The icicles dangle, sharp and bright,
A sparkling dance in morning light.

Through frosted trees, the sun will peek,
A fleeting warmth, yet oh so meek.
In crystal blue, the world unfolds,
A tranquil beauty that never folds.

A palette rich, of white and blue,
With each new glance, a wondrous view.
In nature's frame, we find our peace,
A breath of calm, a sweet release.

The Ethereal Glow of Chilled Mornings

As dawn brings forth a new embrace,
The world is draped in silver lace.
With frosty breath, I greet the day,
In whispered hush, the dreams at play.

The sun peeks through, a gentle tease,
Awakening the slumbering trees.
Each ray a stroke on winter's face,
A soft caress, a warm embrace.

The air is pure, with magic spun,
In every moment, wonder's begun.
With every heartbeat, nature glows,
In chilled embrace, the spirit flows.

The stillness hums a sacred tune,
While shadows stretch toward the moon.
In quiet magic, we unfold,
A story cherished, a tale retold.

So let us bask in morning's light,
Where every whisper feels so right.
In this ethereal dance of time,
We find our hearts in winter's rhyme.

Tales Told by Frozen Streams

Beneath the ice, where shadows dwell,
Whispers linger and stories swell.
The brook is silent, yet speaks so clear,
Of autumn dreams and winter's cheer.

Each ripple trapped, a tale confined,
Of journeys past, by nature designed.
The stones below, in stillness stand,
Guarding secrets of the land.

Frozen murmurs of laughter fade,
In icy grasp, the memories laid.
As seasons change, they softly sigh,
A gentle echo of days gone by.

In winter's hold, it finds its rest,
A dormant time, yet still so blessed.
With every thaw, new hopes arise,
A flowing chorus beneath the skies.

So listen close to the frozen stream,
For in its heart lies every dream.
A tapestry of life and time,
In icy hush, we find our rhyme.

When Silence Enfolds the Earth

When silence wraps the twilight sky,
The whispers fade, a gentle sigh.
Stars blink softly, a distant glow,
In the hush, the heartbeats slow.

Footprints vanish in the white,
As shadows dance in fading light.
Nature's breath, a tranquil balm,
Embraced by peace, a soothing calm.

Around us swirls the quiet night,
Each star a spark, each dream a flight.
In the stillness, hopes take wing,
Await the dawn, what joy will bring?

A world asleep, yet full of dreams,
Where silence flows like gentle streams.
In this moment, all is clear,
In silence, we find what we hold dear.

When silence bids the earth its grace,
We find ourselves in this embrace.
So hold this stillness, make it last,
For in the quiet, we are vast.

Nightfall in a Crystal World

When twilight weaves its velvet thread,
A crystal world beneath us spread.
Moonlight crowns the icy trees,
Painting white with every breeze.

Each flake descends with tender care,
Landscapes glow, a beauty rare.
Stars twinkle in the chill of night,
Transforming shadows into light.

In the stillness, magic stirs,
A symphony of quiet purrs.
Frosty whispers weave through the air,
Creating dreams beyond compare.

Wrapped in blankets, hearts ignite,
In this world, there's pure delight.
Every glance, a wonder told,
A crystal glow, a sight to hold.

Nightfall paints the earth anew,
In hues of silver, shades of blue.
In icy realms, we find our way,
Beneath the stars, we softly sway.

Song of the Icebound Trees

Among the trees, a stillness sings,
Frozen limbs with delicate wings.
Icicles hang like crystal tears,
Nature's lullaby calms our fears.

Branches sway in the winter air,
Whispers echo through the cold glare.
A gentle breath, a fleeting sound,
In this world, solace is found.

Every bough bears a frosted crown,
Glittering softly, majestic gown.
Beneath the weight, they stand so true,
Guardians of dreams, ancient, new.

Listen closely, hear the line,
Nature's secrets, pure and divine.
In every crack, in every seam,
Awakens the heart to dream its dream.

The icebound trees wrap us in grace,
With every pulse, a warm embrace.
Their silent song, a soothing balm,
In their presence, we find calm.

Echoes Through the Moonlit Snow

In moonlit snow, the night unfolds,
Whispers of stories yet untold.
Footsteps echo on the ground,
In every shadow, dreams are found.

A silver glow dances on each flake,
As if the stars themselves awake.
Every breath, a fleeting chance,
In the blanket white, we find our dance.

Voices linger in the chill,
Carving paths through quiet still.
Echoes weave through branches bare,
Carried softly on the air.

The night gazes down, so wise,
Bathed in light from endless skies.
In the hush, our hearts align,
In every whisper, love's design.

Through moonlit snow, we tread with care,
Captured moments hang in air.
With every echo, joy bestows,
A tapestry where magic grows.

Silver Threads in a Pale Landscape

Silver threads weave through the field,
Nature's whispers softly revealed.
In the silence, dreams take flight,
Beneath the cloak of soft moonlight.

Twirling thoughts in gentle sway,
As shadows dance with the end of day.
With every breeze, stories unfold,
Of journeys past, of glories told.

Among the trees, secrets lie still,
Embracing the quiet, the world is thrilled.
Colors fade, yet beauty remains,
In this realm where peace reigns.

A tapestry stitched with care,
Each thread a memory, lightly bare.
Hope emerges in the dawn's embrace,
Brightening the night's solitude space.

Whispers linger, time drifts on,
In a landscape where dreams are drawn.
Silver threads, softly entwined,
In a harmony of heart and mind.

Secrets Held by the Sullen Sky

The sullen sky, a heavy gray,
Hides its secrets, dusk to day.
Beneath the clouds, stories weave,
Of love and loss, of hearts that grieve.

Raindrops fall like silent tears,
Echoing long-forgotten fears.
In shadows cast by fleeting light,
Whispers linger, hidden from sight.

Birds once soared in the endless blue,
Now they seek the skies anew.
Yet beneath the sullen dome,
Lies a heart that dreams of home.

Glimmers of hope in the darkening shade,
The dawn will come, the darkness fade.
Secrets held, but not in vain,
For every storm must break with rain.

In the hush of tempest's breath,
Life's lessons echo, even in death.
The sullen sky, though draped in gray,
Holds the promise of a brighter day.

Beneath the Hush of Snowflakes

Gentle whispers cloak the ground,
In every flake, a world profound.
Beneath the hush of winter's breath,
Lies a canvas, soft as death.

Dreams are painted in pure white,
As day gives way to the quiet night.
Footprints vanish, stories fade,
In the silence, memories wade.

The trees stand tall, cloaked in frost,
In this stillness, nothing is lost.
Winds carry tales from long ago,
In the hush where hope can grow.

Fires crackle, hearts ignite,
In the warmth of the cozy light.
While snowflakes fall in a graceful dance,
Life rewrites each fleeting chance.

Beneath the hush, we find our way,
In the beauty of the winter's sway.
Each moment cherished, each breath a gift,
In the stillness, our spirits lift.

In the Realm of Crystal Light

In the realm where crystals gleam,
Reality merges with a dream.
A tapestry of colors bright,
Dances softly in the light.

Mirrored echoes touch the soul,
Reflecting wonders, making us whole.
Through shimmering paths, we wander free,
In this enchanted reverie.

Glimmers trace the edges of thought,
In the stillness, answers sought.
The world transforms with every gaze,
In the crystal's soft embrace.

Stars collide in a dazzling sway,
Painting night into the day.
A symphony of light does play,
Guiding hearts along the way.

In the realm of crystal light,
Dreams take flight in joyous height.
Each moment sparkles like a star,
In our hearts, we carry far.

Frosted Mirrors of Solitude

In the quiet room, shadows play,
Frosted glass hides the light of day.
Silent thoughts drift in swirling mist,
Memories linger, too soft to resist.

Each breath echoes, a whispered sigh,
Reflections dance as moments fly.
Loneliness wraps like a gentle shroud,
Embracing the heart, tender yet loud.

Days blend softly in shades of gray,
Frosted mirrors keep the world at bay.
In this cocoon of chilly delight,
Solitude glimmers, a star in the night.

Inside the frost, a warmth does bloom,
Hope flickers gently, dispelling the gloom.
With every heartbeat, stories unfold,
In frosted mirrors, the soul we behold.

Through icy panes, the dreams ignite,
Each fragment shimmering, bathed in light.
A dance of spirits on winter's floor,
Frosted mirrors whisper evermore.

Echoes in the Silent Snow

Snowflakes falling, a soft embrace,
Blanketing earth in gentle lace.
Whispers linger where shadows tread,
Echoes of stories, softly spread.

Footsteps muted in winter's grasp,
Each crunch a memory, lost in the past.
Beneath the branches, a world asleep,
In silent snowfall, secrets keep.

A hush blankets all, the air feels thick,
Time slows down, each moment tick.
Echoes in silence, a tranquil hymn,
Nature's canvas, painted dim.

Every flake holds a wish alight,
Drifting slowly through the night.
In this serene, enchanted glow,
A bond is forged in the silent snow.

As dawn approaches, the light will break,
In glistening splendor, a new path to make.
Echoes whisper, a promise to grow,
In the memory of the silent snow.

Chilled Whispers of the Night

Under the stars, where shadows creep,
Chilled whispers call from the depths of sleep.
Moonlight dances on frostbitten ground,
A symphony silent, yet profoundly sound.

Each breeze carries a secret untold,
Flickering fantasies, dreams manifold.
In the stillness, the heart finds space,
Chilled whispers touch with an icy grace.

The night wraps softly like velvet black,
Painting the world with shadows to track.
Stars flicker dimly, a watchful eye,
In the hush of the night, where whispers lie.

As the world sleeps, the spirits play,
In chilled whispers, they drift away.
A tapestry woven of night's sweet sigh,
Each thread a story that will not die.

In twilight's embrace, the heart takes flight,
Chilled whispers beckon, a call to the night.
With every breath, we're drawn to the quest,
In the chilled whispers, we find our rest.

Stillness Beneath the Frozen Sky

Beneath the veil of the frozen sky,
Stillness stretches, a tranquil sigh.
Branches glisten with frost's embrace,
Nature holds still in a silent space.

Clouds drift slowly, obscuring the light,
In this calm moment, everything feels right.
Whispers of winter fill the chill air,
A sacred hush, a heart laid bare.

Footprints scatter on glistening trails,
Each step a story that softly exhales.
Beneath the stars, a promise to keep,
In the stillness, the world's at peace.

Crystals of ice, like dreams on display,
Sparkle and twinkle in night's ballet.
With every heartbeat, life hums and sighs,
Stillness breathes deep beneath frozen skies.

As dawn approaches, the light will fade,
But stillness lingers, a gentle parade.
In nature's embrace, we find our way,
Beneath the frozen, a warm heart will stay.

Solitude in a Snowstorm's Heart

Whispers fall like whispers soft,
Wrapped in a world of pure white.
Silent breaths in frozen time,
Nature's lullaby intertwines.

Amidst the chill, a lone figure,
Wanders through the silent drifts.
Each step a note in winter's song,
Echoing dreams in frosty air.

The sky wears a blanket of gray,
While flakes dance and swirl in delight.
Wrapped in peace, I find my way,
Solitude's warmth, my heart's respite.

Branches bow under heavy peace,
Cocooned in white, the trees stand still.
Snowflakes cradle the evening light,
A tranquil balm on weary hills.

In this moment, time stands still,
The world outside fades to a hush.
In solitude, I meet myself,
In winter's heart, I find my truth.

The Grasp of Deepening Twilight

Crimson hues in the fading light,
Waves of dusk embrace the day.
Shadows stretch, they seem to breathe,
In the grip of twilight's sway.

Stars awaken, shy and slow,
One by one, they fill the sky.
Whispers of night begin to stir,
As soft winds take their gentle sigh.

The moon rises in silver grace,
Casting dreams on the world below.
A canvas painted in soft shades,
As darkness weaves the evening's glow.

What stories hide in this deep hush?
What secrets linger in the air?
The grasp of night holds tight and snug,
Wrapping all in velvet care.

Time drifts softly, like a dream,
In this embrace, all worries cease.
In the twilight's tender arms,
I find a moment filled with peace.

Lattice of Frost on Windowpanes

Artistry etched in frozen breath,
Nature's fingers paint with grace.
A lattice of frost on windowpanes,
Framed reflections of a bright chase.

Each pattern a story untold,
Whispers of joy and silent tears.
Through crystal designs my eyes behold,
The beauty of cold, through the years.

Morning light kisses the frost,
Warming the heart with golden rays.
Each delicate crystal flickers bright,
A dance of light through winter's days.

I trace the lines with curious thought,
Imagining dreams in the chill.
A tapestry of winter's touch,
Inspiring warmth, deep within still.

In the hush of an early morn,
I cherish this fleeting delight.
A lattice of frost, a fleeting truth,
Invites me to pause and take flight.

Glistening Echoes of Solstice Murmurs

When the longest night embraces,
The world in shadows, calm and deep.
Voices of winter softly beckon,
Inviting dreams to drift and seep.

Glistening echoes in the air,
Whispers shared with the darkened trees.
Time slows down as stars emerge,
Carrying secrets on the breeze.

The solstice night wraps all in peace,
Cradling hearts like a gentle song.
In the stillness, a flicker of hope,
The promise of light as nights grow long.

Cinnamon scents and warm embraces,
Stories told by the fireside glow.
In this moment, we connect,
With memories that softly flow.

As dawn approaches, colors ignite,
A palette bright against the gray.
In glistening echoes of murmur's grace,
We welcome the light of a new day.

The Stillness of a Silent Dawn

The world awakens in whispers soft,
As shadows flee from the light above.
A gentle breeze begins to lift,
Embracing all with a tender love.

Birds sing sweetly in the calm,
Each note a promise of the day.
Sunlight dances on dewy grass,
Painting gold along the way.

Mountains stand tall in muted hues,
Wrapped in a cloak of morning mist.
Time stands still in nature's breath,
In this moment, all is kissed.

A symphony of colors bloom,
Filling the sky with a soft embrace.
Nature's palette, pure and bright,
In silence, we find our place.

As day unfolds, so does the peace,
Reflections linger in the air.
The stillness of a silent dawn,
A treasure beyond compare.

Frost's Caress on Nature's Canvas

The trees wear coats of crystal lace,
Each branch adorned with icy beads.
A tranquil world in winter's grace,
Where silence whispers nature's needs.

Fields of white stretch far and wide,
Draped in frost like a silken sheet.
Each step taken with softened stride,
A dance of beauty beneath our feet.

Sunlight sparkles on frozen lakes,
Mirroring dreams in quiet repose.
Nature breathes, a soft heart aches,
For this fleeting moment to forever hold.

Birds trace patterns in the sky,
Their songs a thread of hope and cheer.
In this cold, we seem to fly,
Finding warmth in the atmosphere.

Frost's caress upon the ground,
A masterpiece that time bestows.
In every flake, a wonder found,
Nature's magic, forever flows.

In the Embrace of a Frosty Twilight

The sun dips low, a crimson hue,
As twilight casts its gentle spell.
In frosty air, the world anew,
A silent promise in the swell.

Stars begin to twinkle bright,
While moonbeams weave a silver thread.
Frost entwines the edge of night,
Whispering dreams to be widespread.

The chill unfolds its soft embrace,
Holding close the fading light.
In this moment, nature's grace,
Brings whispers from the encroaching night.

Trees stand still, their secrets kept,
Wrapped in veils of frozen breath.
In this peace, our spirits leapt,
Finding solace in the depths.

As shadows lengthen, silence reigns,
In this cold, we find our spark.
In the embrace of twilight chains,
Hearts ignite and leave their mark.

Ethereal Dreams on Ice

A canvas spread beneath the stars,
Where time seems lost in frozen flow.
Each breath a mist, like whispered bars,
In moonlit dances, spirits glow.

The world feels light, a gentle sigh,
As shimmering frost blankets the ground.
In every flake, a dream to fly,
In ethereal whispers, hope is found.

Beneath the sky, so vast and bright,
A landscape stilled, a silent song.
In these hours of tender night,
We gather dreams where we belong.

Magic swirls in the icy air,
Illuminating hearts aglow.
Each moment cherished, rare and fair,
In this circle, love will grow.

As dawn approaches, dreams will fade,
Yet in our hearts, their warmth remains.
Ethereal moments, softly laid,
In memories where joy still reigns.

The Lullaby of Frozen Nights

In the stillness of the night,
Whispers drift on frosty air.
Moonlight dances, pure and bright,
Crystals spark with gentle flair.

Snowflakes twirl like fleeting dreams,
Wrapped in silence, soft and white.
Stars above, in silver beams,
Watch as shadows hug the night.

A lullaby of winter's breath,
Cradles hearts in tender peace.
In this haven, fears find death,
As the world begins to cease.

Hushed in beauty's frozen grace,
Every moment holds its breath.
Time slows down in this embrace,
Where dreams linger, free from death.

As I wander through the chill,
Nature wraps me in her glow.
Every heartbeat, every thrill,
Sings the love that winter shows.

Frostbitten Dreams Under Starry Skies

Underneath the starry skies,
Dreams awaken, cold and bright.
Frostbitten whispers, soft goodbyes,
Carried gently through the night.

Moonbeams drape the trees in white,
Woven tales of ice and fire.
In the heart of frozen light,
Yearning stirs our deep desire.

A canvas of the midnight blue,
Painted with the dawn's embrace.
Frosted dreams begin anew,
In this quiet, sacred space.

Every sigh a cloud of mist,
Every heartbeat, calm and slow.
In this moment, none are missed,
As the night begins to glow.

Stars like jewels, twinkling bright,
Guide us through the wintry chill.
We will hold this tranquil sight,
In our hearts, a timeless thrill.

Silent Footfalls on Powdered Ground

In the night, soft echoes sound,
Silent footfalls on powdered ground.
Each in step, the world unwinds,
Tales of wonder, nature finds.

Footprints leave a fleeting trace,
Our small secrets in this space.
Through the whiteness, whispers flow,
Hidden meadows start to glow.

Stillness cloaks the frozen trees,
Nature's breath, a gentle freeze.
In the night, a song discreet,
Harmonies that gently meet.

Snowflakes kiss the earth with grace,
Every moment finds its place.
Footfalls vanish, lost in time,
Leaving echoes, soft and mime.

Beneath the veil of winter's night,
Every heartbeat feels so right.
In the silence, dreams are found,
In the whispers all around.

Fragments of a Still Hearth

By the hearth, the embers glow,
Fragments of warmth in the cold.
Stories linger, soft and slow,
Whispers of the hearth, we're told.

Shadows dance upon the wall,
Flickering with tales of old.
Each flame rises, fragile call,
Binding us in truth, so bold.

Memories wrapped in twilight's hue,
Embers flicker, fade away.
In the calm, a quiet view,
As night turns to gentle day.

Through the glass, the snowflakes fall,
Nature's quiet, softest sigh.
In this circle, we stand tall,
Finding peace as moments fly.

Fragments heal, and hearts align,
As we gather, lost in time.
In this space, our lives entwine,
By the hearth, our love will climb.

Chasing the Light of Shortened Days

As autumn leaves begin to fall,
The golden sun bids us farewell.
We chase the light, across the hall,
In shadows deep, our stories dwell.

The days grow short, the nights extend,
We gather warmth in twilight's glow.
With every breath, our hopes descend,
In fleeting time, we strive to grow.

Embrace the chill, the crisp embrace,
With newfound strength, the heart ignites.
We'll weave our dreams through time and space,
And chase the light as day turns nights.

A fleeting dance, as seasons turn,
With whispered winds, they guide our way.
In every spark, our passions burn,
As we chase light in shorter days.

Though darkness falls, together we stand,
Bound by the warmth of love's bright glow.
Our spirits soar, hand in hand,
Chasing the light, through every woe.

Stuffed Skies and Fallen Stars

The heavens brimmed with untold dreams,
A tapestry of wishes sewn.
But in the night, a silence screams,
As fallen stars turn into stone.

The clouds, they stretch, a heavy quilt,
Stuffed with secrets, shadows cast.
Each droplet holds the dreams we built,
Yet in their wake, our hopes drift past.

We raise our heads, and fear awakes,
For every star that fades to gray.
In the abyss, our courage shakes,
As stuffed skies swallow light away.

Still, hearts alight with embered fire,
We seek the stars that slipped away.
With every breath, we dare aspire,
To claim the night, come what may.

Through darkened skies, our dreams take flight,
In cosmic depths, we find our scars.
A dance of loss, of love, of light,
In stuffed skies and fallen stars.

The Lull of the Longest Night

As night descends, the world grows still,
A hush surrounds, a tender balm.
The moonlight casts a gentle thrill,
In shadows deep, we find our calm.

The chill in air, a crisp embrace,
With whispered tales of dreams long gone.
In every shadow, we find grace,
As time drifts softly, drawn along.

The stars above, in quiet gleam,
Like echoes of our past's delight.
A lullaby, a timeless theme,
Resounds beneath the longest night.

With every breath, we drift away,
In quiet moments, thoughts take flight.
A promise made, we long to stay,
Wrapped in the lull of gentle night.

As dawn approaches, shadows fade,
But in our hearts, the stillness clings.
In every memory, love is laid,
The lull of night, where dreaming sings.

A Portrait in Ice

In frozen stillness, time suspends,
A world encased in crystal light.
Each fleeting glance, a moment blends,
A portrait forged, in winter's bite.

The branches draped in diamond dust,
Reflects the sun's soft, golden gleam.
We breathe in whispers, that we trust,
In silence, we shape every dream.

Each drop of frost, a tale untold,
A memory held in icy grasp.
In winter's hold, so fierce yet bold,
We find our hearts in nature's clasp.

A moment's pause, to gaze and be,
Immortalized in time's embrace.
With every breath, the soul can see,
The beauty wrapped in nature's grace.

In landscapes carved from dreams of ice,
We wander paths of fleeting light.
A portrait drawn, both sharp and nice,
In frozen realms, our spirits take flight.

Erased Footsteps in Shimmering White

The world wraps in a blanket bright,
Each step fades into the quiet night.
Whispers of winter softly call,
Memories linger, yet not at all.

Hushed tones settle, shadows sweep,
Footprints vanish, secrets keep.
Softly glistening in the moon's glow,
Nature sings the tales we know.

Sky above in velvet deep,
Stars like dreams, in silence sleep.
The breath of frost, a gentle sigh,
Every echo bids goodbye.

Mountains cradle the winter's breath,
Carving stillness, touching death.
In this solace, winter's grace,
Erased footsteps leave no trace.

Daylight beckons, yet stays shy,
While twilight drapes the earth nearby.
In shimmering white, the world unfolds,
A thousand stories left untold.

The Hidden Dance of Snowflakes

In the sky, a ballet's spun,
Delicate twirls, a dance begun.
No two alike in their flight,
Each one whispers, pure delight.

Graceful forms in the calm air,
Twinkling jewels without a care.
They drift and sway in soft embrace,
Nature's rhythm, a gentle pace.

Quiet laughter in the chill,
A soft hush, all time stands still.
Crystalline wonders weave and dive,
In their chaos, dreams arrive.

They find their home on earth's warm cheek,
Painting silence, a language unique.
With every fall, a story told,
A hidden dance, a sight to behold.

As sunlight kisses each design,
Sparkling whispers, divine align.
Beneath the heavens' vast expanse,
We find our joy in the snowflakes' dance.

Veiled Sunlight in a Frozen Dream

Morning light through branches weaves,
The world shimmers as winter breathes.
Pale hues wrap the trees so tight,
Veiled sunlight in a frozen sight.

Softly glowing, the world anew,
Lost in wonder, the old feels true.
In the stillness, time sings sweet,
Frozen dreams beneath our feet.

Branches heavy, stooping low,
Veils of frost in silver glow.
Whispers carried on the breeze,
In nature's quiet, hearts find ease.

A golden hue breaks the dawn,
Painting the edges of the lawn.
Each beam dances with gentle grace,
In frozen dreams, we find our place.

With every heartbeat, warmth returns,
Through hidden sunlight, our spirit burns.
In the chill, beauty finds its seam,
Wrapped in the veil of a frozen dream.

Solstice Songs Beneath the Snow

The darkest night holds secrets deep,
In slumber's hush, the world does keep.
Solstice songs in whispers glide,
Beneath the snow, pure hearts confide.

Stars glimmering, a distant choir,
Melodies born from winter's fire.
In every flake, a note unfolds,
Tales of warmth in the bitter cold.

Underneath a quilt of white,
The earth breathes softly, wrapped in light.
Frozen echoes tenderly sway,
As dreams awaken at break of day.

Crisp air sings of branches bare,
While shadows dance without a care.
Each breath of frost a gentle kiss,
Solstice songs, a fleeting bliss.

As the sun returns its glow,
Joy awakens beneath the snow.
In this silence, hope takes wing,
Beneath the snow, the heart will sing.

A Dance of Shadows on White Canvas

In twilight's hush, they twirl and sway,
As whispers paint the night to day.
Their movements blend in graceful flight,
A dance of shadows, pure delight.

On canvas stretched, the colors play,
In gentle strokes, they drift away.
Each shadow bends, a fleeting phase,
An artform born of night's embrace.

With laughter soft, they intertwine,
A tapestry of hearts aligned.
Beneath the stars, the dreams unspool,
In every trace, the night's own jewel.

The moonlight casts a silken shade,
Where fantasies and truths are laid.
A dance unfolds, the echoes ring,
In shadows deep, the night takes wing.

As dawn approaches, colors blend,
The shadows bow, their time to end.
Yet in our hearts, their essence stays,
A memory of twilight's ways.

Fading Footprints in the Snow

Upon the ground, a tale is told,
Of dreams once chased, of hopes so bold.
Each footprint marks a moment passed,
In winter's grasp, they fade so fast.

The chilly air, a silent friend,
As daylight wanes, the shadows bend.
The snowflakes fall, a soft embrace,
Concealing paths, erasing trace.

Where laughter rang, a whisper sighs,
Beneath the weight of winter skies.
Each step a memory, sweet and light,
Now cloaked in white, hidden from sight.

Yet in the heart, the warmth remains,
Of all the joy, the love, the pains.
Though footprints fade, some truths abide,
In quiet corners, they still hide.

The chill of dusk, the twilight glow,
Reminds us of the paths we know.
With every storm, new layers grow,
Yet hearts still beat beneath the snow.

Ember Glow in the Frostbitten Glow

Amidst the chill, the embers dance,
A flicker bright, a daring chance.
Each spark a story, warm and slow,
In winter's breath, the softest glow.

Beneath the frost, a fire breathes,
As shadows weave through frozen leaves.
The world is still, the night is deep,
But in the hearth, the memories leap.

With every crackle, tales unfold,
Of summer's warmth and nights of gold.
While frosty winds cut like a knife,
The ember glow ignites our life.

Outside it bites, the cold takes hold,
But inside round, we brave the cold.
We gather close, with hearts aglow,
While winter wraps the world in snow.

And so we sit as shadows loom,
In ember's glow, dispelling gloom.
The frost may chill, but here we know,
Together we will face the flow.

The Solace of Frosty Evenings

In frosty evenings, still and bright,
The world is draped in soft moonlight.
Each breath exhaled, a cloud of white,
A tranquil hush, the heart takes flight.

The trees stand tall, adorned in lace,
While stars peek down, their twinkling grace.
A canvas vast, where dreams can roam,
These frosty nights feel just like home.

With every step, the crunch of frost,
A gentle march, no moment lost.
The stillness wraps us, calm and true,
In winter's hold, our spirits grew.

The air is crisp, the night profound,
In quiet moments, peace is found.
As cold winds weave through silent trees,
The heart finds solace, sweet as these.

So let the frost embrace the night,
With every star, our dreams take flight.
In frosty evenings, we unite,
Wrapped in the warmth of shared light.

Beneath the Veil of Glacial Light

Chilled whispers dance on frozen air,
Veils of ice weave tales of despair.
Stars shimmer softly in the night,
Guided by the glacial light.

Moonlit shadows stretch and sigh,
While secrets quiet in the sky.
Each flake falls with a gentle grace,
A tapestry of time and space.

Hoarfrost clings to branches bare,
Nature's breath, a silent prayer.
Glistening trails the stillness keep,
In the heart where secrets sleep.

The world is hushed, a tranquil scene,
Echoes caught in silver sheen.
Beneath the veil, the night takes flight,\nWrapped in the
arms of glacial light.

In this realm of frozen dreams,
A symphony of crystal beams.
Each moment frozen, yet alive,
Beneath the veil, the spirits thrive.

Reflections in the Frosted Pond

A silver disk beneath the trees,
Whispers carried by the breeze.
Frozen glass, a mirror bright,
Holds the echoes of daylight.

Ripples linger in the cold,
Stories of the brave and bold.
Beneath the ice, life stirs anew,
A hidden world, a tranquil view.

Trees stand guard, their branches white,
Time unfolds in soft twilight.
Each breath of wind a gentle song,
In this space where dreams belong.

Reflections twist and gracefully play,
Echoing the colors of the day.
In the silence, peace is found,
In the frosted pond's embrace, we're bound.

As twilight falls, the shadows grow,
In the stillness, the secrets flow.
A world transformed, serene and grand,
Reflections shimmering, hand in hand.

The Heart of Silence Cradled in Cold

In the quiet, silence reigns,
Wrapped in freezing, gentle chains.
Snowflakes whisper, softly fall,
The heartbeat of the stillness calls.

Each breath of frost, a fleeting sigh,
Underneath the vast, dark sky.
Crisp air fills the void with grace,
In the heart where shadows embrace.

Winter's blanket soft and deep,
Cradling dreams that gently sleep.
In the still, a world's refrain,
The pulse of life in icy veins.

Amid the snow, the stars appear,
Glistening dreams, the night draws near.
In the heart of cold's gentle hold,
A story waits, yet to unfold.

The silence swells, a sacred space,
Finding warmth in winter's face.
Here in the depths, a light is found,
The heart of silence, wrapped around.

Paths Woven by Silver Light

Luminescent trails weave through night,
Guiding footsteps with silver light.
Each star a thread in dark's embrace,
Tracing paths through time and space.

Moonlight dances on the snow,
Gentle whispers, soft and slow.
Letting go of what we know,
As dreams unfurl, like petals show.

Gathered here, where shadows blend,
Each moment bends, as feelings mend.
Woven whispers in the chill,
A tapestry shaped by the will.

Through the frosted trees we roam,
Finding in the stillness, home.
With every step, the night ignites,
Our journey marked by silver lights.

Paths entwined in nature's art,
Echoing the beat of heart.
In this quiet, we unite,
Following paths woven by silver light.

The Heart of a Frozen Stream

Beneath the ice, the water flows,
A secret song, the current knows.
Silent whispers, tales untold,
In winter's grasp, the dreams unfold.

Snowflakes dance on crystal skies,
Reflecting light, the beauty lies.
Nature's chill, yet warmth remains,
In frozen realms, the heart sustains.

Branches bow with frosty grace,
Nature's breath, a gentle trace.
Time stands still, the world awaits,
As spring arrives to mend the fates.

Bubbles trapped in icy art,
Echoes of a beating heart.
Forever held in winter's clime,
A promise kept through pulse of time.

When thawing sun begins to shine,
The flowing stream will intertwine.
Awakening from winter's dream,
Revealing all, the heart redeemed.

Frozen Over Dreams

In twilight hours, shadows play,
Dreams entombed in ice, they stay.
Whispers linger, memories freeze,
A haunting calm, a silent tease.

Stars above, like diamonds bright,
Glisten softly in the night.
Frozen hopes, but never lost,
Awaiting spring, whatever cost.

In stillness lies the promise kept,
Of dreams once dreamt, of tears wept.
With every flake, a wish enclosed,
In winter's breath, the heart opposed.

Yet in the dark, a spark will glow,
A hint of warmth, a gentle flow.
From frozen depths, a fire ignites,
Igniting souls on starry nights.

As seasons shift and time aligns,
The ice will melt, the heart refines.
From frozen dreams, a bloom will stir,
When springtime comes, our hearts confer.

A Hushed Prelude to Spring

Whispers soft upon the breeze,
Winter yields with gentle ease.
The world awaits with bated breath,
In quietude, we dance with death.

Among the snowdrops, life begins,
A melody that softly spins.
With every thaw, a vibrant hue,
A prelude bright, the old anew.

Nature's pulse, a subtle sound,
From hibernation, life unbound.
The warmth ascends, the chill must go,
In tender grace, the blossoms grow.

Birds return to serenade,
A symphony that will not fade.
In every note, a life reborn,
Hushed hope awakens with the dawn.

As dawn breaks clear, the sky turns gold,
A tale of spring begins to unfold.
We welcome warmth, a sweet embrace,
In nature's dance, we find our place.

The Crystal Ballet of Nature

Where sunlight meets the icy ground,
A ballet swirls, elegant and sound.
Each flake a dancer, pure and bright,
In nature's stage, a frozen delight.

Branches sway, adorned in white,
Nature's grace in frosty light.
The world transformed, a crystal sheen,
A masterpiece, serene and keen.

With every gust, the dancers twirl,
In shimmering robes, they twist and swirl.
Beneath the moon, they take their flight,
A silent echo of pure delight.

In every glint, a story spun,
Of life beneath the winter sun.
With each soft note of winter's song,
A tale of beauty, pure and strong.

As seasons change, the ballet ends,
Yet in our hearts, the magic blends.
For nature's grace is never far,
In every breath, a shining star.

Frosted Whispers

Whispers travel on the breeze,
Softly dancing through the trees.
Every flake a story told,
As the world turns white and cold.

In the hush of winter's night,
Moonlight bathes in silver light.
Footprints vanish, secrets steep,
In the silence, stillness deep.

Nature holds its breath in peace,
Worries fade and troubles cease.
In the crisp, the heart finds grace,
In the frosted, sweet embrace.

Stars above like diamonds gleam,
Frozen lakes reflect a dream.
Magic glimmers, beauty shines,
In the air, serenity aligns.

Beneath a quilt of snow so white,
Sleep brings warmth through the cold night.
In this realm of soft repose,
Frosted whispers gently close.

Echoes in a Snowbound Silence

Silent snowfall blankets all,
Nature's hush, a gentle call.
Footsteps crunch on frosty ground,
In this peace, lost thoughts are found.

Icicles hang like crystal tears,
Stories breathed into the years.
Echoes linger, soft and low,
In the heart where dreams can grow.

Whirling winds in winter's song,
Softly murmur, right or wrong.
Voices trapped in frosted air,
Whispers woven everywhere.

Time stands still in snowy light,
Holding moments, pure and bright.
Within this calm, reflections play,
As echoes fade and drift away.

A world adorned in silver sheen,
Where every shadow feels serene.
In the grasp of winter's night,
Echoes blend with pure delight.

Chilling Embrace of Time

Frigid air wraps 'round the soul,
Moments freeze as they unfold.
Time, a river turned to ice,
Chilling whispers, cold as spice.

Fingers touch the frosted glass,
Marks of life like shadows pass.
In the stillness, stories dwell,
Silent secrets, truths to tell.

Glimmers flicker in the dark,
Hope ignites a tiny spark.
Chill embraces every line,
As the heart begins to pine.

Melodies of winter play,
In the crisp, the dreams delay.
Every breath a cloud of white,
In this haunting, frozen night.

Embrace the cold, find solace near,
For time, though chill, brings warmth sincere.
Underneath the ice, love glows,
In chilling exchanges, life flows.

Icy Stillness and Shimmering Light

Through the trees, the shadows creep,
Icy stillness whispers deep.
Glimmers dance on fields so bright,
Shimmering beneath the night.

Every flake a miracle dear,
Crafted by the frost's fierce spear.
Nature sleeps, yet dreams awake,
In the stillness, hearts partake.

Crystal rivers cease their flow,
Lands embraced in icy glow.
Shimmering stars like lanterns gleam,
In the quiet, we can dream.

Frosting covers branches bare,
Whisper soft in the chilled air.
All the world in quiet light,
Holds the promise of delight.

In the calm, find solace new,
A shimmering world to wander through.
In icy stillness, warmth ignites,
Life enjoys its frosty sights.

Serene Hues of the Hibernal Breeze

Gentle whispers through the pines,
Casting shadows, soft, divine.
Blankets white on emerald ground,
Peaceful silence all around.

Frosty breath in morning light,
Turning earth to diamond bright.
Nature sleeps in tender grace,
Winter's kiss on every face.

Crisp the air, a cooling sigh,
Echoes of the sparrows fly.
Amid the chill, a soft embrace,
Serenity in this quiet place.

Footsteps crunch on powdery snow,
Among the trees where moonlight glows.
Each branch adorned, a silver crest,
In this season, we find rest.

Evening falls, the skies transform,
Stars emerge, a cosmic norm.
Underneath the sky so vast,
Whispers of the night are cast.

Winter's Lullaby in a Frozen World

Softly sings the winter night,
Chill and warm, a dance of light.
Underneath the silver moon,
Nature hums a frozen tune.

Icicles hang with delicate grace,
Painting scenes in cold embrace.
Whispers of the softly falling,
Snowflakes in the silence calling.

Trees adorned in frosty lace,
Slowly swaying, a gentle pace.
All is still, the world a dream,
Nestled in the soothing theme.

In the quiet of the hour,
Winter holds a magic power.
Tucked in warmth by hearth's soft glow,
Winds now sing of tales long ago.

Close your eyes and drift away,
To the land where shadows play.
In the lull of winter's breath,
Find the peace that conquers death.

Mirage of Warmth in Chilling Air

Beneath the frost, a spark of heat,
Mirage flickers, soft and sweet.
In the air where cold winds twine,
Hope arises, brightly shine.

Fires dance in amber hues,
Chasing off the winter blues.
Beneath the stars, the laughter flows,
Together in the warmth we chose.

Sips of cider, sweet and spiced,
Chasing chills that once enticed.
Gathered close, our breaths entwined,
In this warmth, we will find.

Glimmers of sun through snowflakes gleam,
In this moment, we believe.
Magic lingers in the air,
As we dream without a care.

Though the tempests rage and play,
We will find a brighter way.
In the heart of winter's night,
Mirage gleams with purest light.

Unseen Traces of Luminous Frost

Glistening trails where shadows creep,
In the night, the world's asleep.
Frosty patterns, etched with care,
Nature's art is always there.

Moonlight kisses every hill,
In the quiet, all is still.
Crystal whispers, soft and clear,
Carrying secrets, drawing near.

Each breath visible, a danced art,
In this realm, winter's heart.
Fleeting moments, fleeting light,
Unseen traces of the night.

Beauty lies in every flake,
In the calm, the frost awakes.
Drawing lines on windowpanes,
Winter's touch, it softly reigns.

Endless frost, unyielding grace,
In its hold, we find our place.
In these traces, silence found,
Harmony in frosty ground.

In the Quiet Embrace of Frost

In the pale of morning light,
Frost blankets all in white,
Whispers chill the waking dawn,
Nature's breath, a quiet yawn.

Branches lace with silver thread,
A dance where frozen dreams are fed,
Each crystal spark a quiet song,
In this embrace, where hearts belong.

Footprints trace the frozen ground,
In solitude, a peace profound,
Every step a story shared,
In the stillness, love declared.

Ice adorns the world so bright,
A canvas touched by winter's might,
In tranquil hues, the moments freeze,
Time holds its breath in quiet ease.

As the sun slips down the sky,
Shadows stretch and softly sigh,
In the dark, the frost remains,
A gentle heart that never wanes.

Harmonies of Cosmic Chill

Stars embrace the midnight sky,
A symphony of dreams awry,
Cosmic whispers, secrets told,
In the chill, the night turns gold.

Galaxies in frozen dance,
Swirling in a cosmic trance,
Every twinkle sings of time,
In the cold, a mystic rhyme.

Planets sing their timeless tune,
Beneath the watchful silver moon,
Echoes of a thousand nights,
In the dark, the heart ignites.

Nebulas blush with frosty hues,
Painting skies with vivid views,
In the silence, beauty blooms,
A tapestry of glowing rooms.

In this realm, where cold winds blow,
The universe begins to flow,
Each heartbeat, a celestial leap,
In cosmic chill, we quietly sleep.

Hibernation in the Cold Light

Beneath the blanket, creatures lie,
In dreams where silent whispers sigh,
As winter's grip holds fast the earth,
The world awaits a warmer birth.

Cozy nooks where shadows play,
Time stretches on, a gentle sway,
In the stillness, hearts take flight,
Hiding from the cold light.

Winds may howl, but peace remains,
As nature wears her frozen chains,
In every nook, a secret kept,
In hibernation, souls have slept.

Through icy nights, long shadows creep,
Silent vigil, a timeless sleep,
Beneath the frost, life stirs anew,
Whispers of spring, the sky so blue.

In this cold, the stories weave,
Of life and hope, we all believe,
As winter fades, we'll rise and sing,
From hibernation, welcoming spring.

Treading the Snow's Whispering Tongue

Softly falling, quiet grace,
Snowflakes dance in frosty lace,
Whispers echo through the glade,
In the hush, our fears evade.

Footprints mark the untamed trail,
With every step, the soft winds wail,
Nature's voice, a song so clear,
In the snow, we feel no fear.

Frosted trees, guardians bold,
Stand in silence, tales unfold,
Every shadow, each point of light,
Guides us through the winter night.

The world transformed, a crystal dream,
Frozen rivers, a shimmering stream,
We tread softly, hearts aligned,
In this magic, peace we find.

As dawn breaks, a gentle glow,
Awakens life beneath the snow,
In every flake, the whispers sing,
Of warmth to come, the joy of spring.

Encompassed by the Chill of Time

The frost it clings, a silent ghost,
Memories linger, shadows so close.
The clock ticks slow, a whispered sigh,
Each moment held, as days drift by.

In winter's grasp, the world turns white,
Silent echoes dance in the night.
Underneath stars, the cold winds blow,
Time sits still, in a tranquil glow.

Through icy fingers, warmth recedes,
In stillness found, our heart's true needs.
Yet hope resounds, a distant chime,
We find our way, in the chill of time.

Beneath the skies, where silence reigns,
We wander paths marked by our pains.
Yet in each breath, we forge ahead,
For life endures where joys have fled.

Embraced by moments, lost yet near,
We walk through seasons, shed our fear.
In every chill, a spark ignites,
A promise born in winter nights.

Glistening Memories Beneath Ice

A glimmer soft, on frozen ground,
The past awaits, in hues profound.
Each breath a cloud, a tender trace,
In quiet morn, find warmth and grace.

Reflections twinkle, as time stands still,
Caught in a net of winter's chill.
Beneath the frost, a story lies,
Of laughter shared beneath the skies.

We walk with care, on fragile dreams,
Where glistening hope flows in soft streams.
Each step reveals, forgotten lore,
In lands of ice, we seek for more.

The world adorned in shimmering white,
Speaks of the tales that share the night.
With every breath, we weave our song,
Beneath the ice, we still belong.

As seasons shift, the thaw will come,
But memories stay, a beating drum.
In every glimmer, a spark ignites,
A journey bright, in winter's nights.

Twilight's Embrace in a Silver Landscape

At twilight's touch, the world aglow,
A silver sheen on the hills below.
The sun dips low, a gentle sigh,
Embracing shadows as stars draw nigh.

The trees stand tall, in still repose,
In whispered winds, their secret flows.
The sky adorned in softest hues,
Where dreams take flight, and hearts renew.

Amongst the calm, a peace descends,
The twilight hour, where time suspends.
In every breath, the night unfolds,
A tapestry of stories told.

With silver light, the world transforms,
In twilight's arms, our spirit warms.
Under the cloak of night we roam,
In every glance, we feel at home.

As stars emerge, we take our place,
In the quiet beauty, we find grace.
In twilight's embrace, all fears dissolve,
In silver landscapes, our hearts evolve.

Solitary Footprints in the Snow

A lone path carved in soft white snow,
Tells of a journey, where few dare go.
Each print a whisper, a tale to tell,
Of dreams once born, in winter's swell.

The chill it bites, yet warmth remains,
In solitude found, we break our chains.
Each step we take, a choice we make,
In snowy fields, our hearts awake.

The world in hush, as shadows grow,
Embracing silence where soft winds blow.
With every footfall, the past retreats,
In landscapes bright, the spirit greets.

We wander forth, into the unknown,
With every breath, we aren't alone.
For in the snow, our stories blend,
In solitude's grace, we find a friend.

As stars ignite in the vast expanse,
We lose ourselves in a daring dance.
Solitary footprints, yet hearts entwined,
In snowy realms, our souls defined.

Milton Keynes UK
Ingram Content Group UK Ltd.
UKHW010230111224
452348UK00011B/629